Amazing Grace!

A selection of favourite hymns based on the Bible.

Read God's Word
and Praise His Name!

1. Abide with me

Abide with me : fast falls the eventide;
The darkness deepens; Lord, with me abide;
When other helpers fail, and comforts flee,
Help of the helpless, O abide with me.

Swift to its close ebbs out life's little day;
Earth's joys grow dim, its glories pass away;
Change and decay in all around I see;
O Thou who changest not, abide with me.

I need Thy presence every passing hour;
What but Thy grace can foil the tempter's power?
Who like Thyself my guide and stay can be?
Through cloud and sunshine, O abide with me.

I fear no foe, with Thee at hand to bless;
Ills have no weight, and tears no bitterness;
Where is death's sting? Where, grave, thy victory?
I triumph still if Thou abide with me.

Hold Thou Thy Cross before my closing eyes,
Shine through the gloom, and point me to the skies;
Heaven's morning breaks, and earth's vain shadows flee:
In life and death, O Lord, abide with me.

"I will not be afraid, Lord, for you are with me."

"Stay with us; the day is almost over and it is getting dark."

Luke 24 v29.

"Listen! I stand at the door and knock; if anyone hears my voice and opens the door, I will come into his house and eat with him, and he will eat with me."

Revelation 3 v 20.

"Jesus answered, 'Whoever loves me will obey my teaching. My Father will love him, and my Father and I will come to him and live with him.'"

John 14 v 23.

"Even though I go through the deepest darkness, I will not be afraid, Lord, for you are with me. Your shepherd's rod and staff protect me."

Psalm 23 v 4.

2. Amazing Grace

Amazing grace - how sweet the sound -
that saves a wretch like me!
I once was lost, but now I'm found,
was blind, but now I see.

'Twas grace that taught my heart to fear,
and grace those fears relieved;
how precious did that grace appear
the hour I first believed.

Through many dangers, toils and snares,
I have already come;
'tis grace that brought me safe thus far,
and grace will lead me home.

When we've been there ten thousand years
bright shining as the sun,
we've no less days to sing God's praise
than when we've first begun.

"God's mercy is so abundant"

"God's mercy is so abundant, and his love for us is so great, that while we were spiritually dead in our disobedience he brought us to life in Christ.

It is by God's grace you have been saved. In our union with Christ Jesus he raised us up with him to rule with him in the heavenly world. He did this to demonstrate for all time the extraordinary greatness of his grace in the love he showed us in Christ Jesus.

For it is by God's grace that you have been saved through faith. It is not the result of your own efforts, but God's gift, so that no one can boast about it. God has made us what we are, and in our union with Christ Jesus he has created us for a life of good deeds, which he has already prepared for us to do."

Ephesians 2 v 4 - 10.

3. At the name of Jesus

At the name of Jesus
Every knee shall bow,
Every tongue confess Him
King of Glory now;
'Tis the Father's pleasure
We should call Him Lord,
Who from the beginning
Was the mighty Word.

Humbled for a season,
To receive a name,
From the lips of sinners,
Unto whom he came,
Faithfully He bore it,
Spotless to the last,
Brought it back victorious,
When from death He passed.

Name Him, brothers, name
Him
With love strong as death,
But with awe and wonder
And with bated breath!
He is God the Saviour,
He is Christ the Lord,
Ever to be worshipped,
Trusted and adored.

In your hearts enthrone Him;
There let Him subdue
All that is not holy,
All that is not true;
Crown Him as your Captain
In temptation's hour;
Let His will enfold you
In its might and power.

Brothers, this Lord Jesus
Shall return again,
With his Father's glory,
And His angel train;
For all wreaths of empire
Meet upon His brow,
And our hearts confess Him
King of Glory now.

"Jesus Christ is Lord"

"The attitude you should have is the one the Lord Jesus had:

He always had the nature of God, but he did not think that by force he should try to become equal with God.

Instead of this, of his own free will he gave up all he had, and took the nature of a servant.

He became like man and appeared in human likeness. He was obedient and walked the path of obedience all the way to death - his death on the cross.

For this reason God raised him to the highest place above and gave him the name that is greater than any other name. And so, in honour of the name of Jesus all beings in heaven, on the earth, and in the world below will fall on their knees, and all will openly proclaim that Jesus Christ is Lord, to the glory of God the Father."

Philippians 2 v 5 - 11.

4. Beneath the Cross of Jesus

Beneath the Cross of Jesus
I fain would take my stand -
The shadow of a mighty rock
Within a weary land;
A home within a wilderness,
A rest upon the way,
From the burning of the noontide heat
And the burden of the day.

O safe and happy shelter,
O refuge tried and sweet,
O trysting place where heaven's love
And heaven's justice meet!
As to the exiled patriarch
That wondrous dream was given
So seems my Saviour's Cross to me -
A ladder up to heaven.

Upon that Cross of Jesus,
Mine eye at times can see
The very dying form of one
Who suffered there for me;
And from my smitten heart, with tears,
Two wonders I confess -
The wonder of His glorious love,
And my own worthlessness.

I take, O Cross, thy shadow
For my abiding place;
I ask no other sunshine than
The sunshine of His face;
Content to let the world go by,
To know no gain nor loss -
My sinful self my only shame,
My glory, all the Cross.

"This is the hour"

"When anyone is joined to Christ, he is a new being; the old has gone, the new has come. All this is done by God, who through Christ Jesus changed us from enemies into his friends and gave us the task of making others his friends also. Our message is that God was making all mankind his friends through Christ. God did not keep an account of their sins, and he has given us the message which tells how he makes them his friends.

Here we are, then, speaking for Christ, as though God himself were making his appeal through us. We plead with you on Christ's behalf : let God change you from enemies into his friends! Christ was without sin, but for our sake God made him share our sin in order that in union with him we might share the righteousness of God.

In our work together with God, then, we beg you who have received God's grace not to let it be wasted. Hear what God says :

'When the time came for me to show you favour I heard you; when the day arrived for me to save you I helped you.'

Listen! This is the hour to receive God's favour; today is the day to be saved!"

2 Corinthians 5 v 17 - 6 v 2.

5. Come, Holy Spirit, come

Come, Holy Spirit, come;
Let Thy bright beams arise;
Dispel the darkness from our minds,
And open all our eyes.

Cheer our desponding hearts,
Thou heavenly Paraclete;
Give us to lie with humble hope
At our Redeemer's feet.

Revive our drooping faith;
Our doubts and fears remove;
And kindle in our breasts the flame
Of never-dying love.

Convince us of our sin;
Then lead to Jesus blood,
And to our wondering view reveal
The secret love of God.

'Tis Thine to cleanse the heart,
To sanctify the soul,
To pour fresh life on every part,
And new create the whole.

Dwell, therefore, in our hearts;
Our minds from bondage free;
Then shall we know and praise and love
The Father, Son and Thee.

"Another Helper"

Jesus said, "If you love me, you will obey my commandments. I will ask the Father, and he will give you another Helper, who will stay with you for ever. He is the Spirit who reveals the truth about God. The world cannot receive him, because it cannot see him or know him. But you know him, because he remains with you and is in you.

"When I go, you will not be left all alone; I will come back to you. In a little while the world will see me no more, but you will see me; and because I live, you also will live. When that day comes, you will know that I am in my Father and that you are in me, just as I am in you."

John 14 v 15 - 19.

6. Crown Him with many crowns

Crown Him with many crowns,
The Lamb upon His throne:
Hark how the heavenly anthem drowns
All music but its own.
Awake, my soul and sing
Of Him who died for thee,
And hail him as thy matchless King
Through all eternity.

Crown Him the Lord of life
Who triumphed o'er the grave,
And rose victorious in the strife
For those He came to save.
His glories now we sing
Who died and rose on high,
Who died eternal life to bring
And lives that death may die.

Crown Him the Lord of peace,
Whose power a sceptre sways
From pole to pole, that wars may cease,
Absorbed in prayer and praise.
His reign shall know no end;
And round His pierced feet
Fair flowers of paradise extend
Their fragrance ever sweet.

Crown Him the Lord of love;
Behold His hands and side,
Rich wounds yet visible above,
In beauty glorified.
All hail, Redeemer, hail!
For Thou hast died for me;
Thy praise shall never, never fail
Throughout eternity.

"You are worthy"

"The Lamb went and took the scroll from the right hand of the one who sits on the throne. As he did so, the four living creatures and the twenty-four elders fell down before the Lamb... They sang a new song :

'You are worthy to take the scroll and to break open its seals. For you were killed, and by your sacrificial death you bought for God people from every tribe, language, nation, and race. You have made them a kingdom of priests to serve our God, and they shall rule on earth.'

Again I looked, and I heard angels, thousands and millions of them! They stood round the throne, the four living creatures, and the elders, and sang in a loud voice:

'The Lamb that was killed is worthy to receive power, wealth, wisdom, and strength, honour, glory, and praise!' And I heard every creature in heaven, on earth, in the world below, and in the sea - all living beings in the universe - and they were singing :

'To him who sits on the throne and to the Lamb, be praise and honour, glory and might, for ever and ever!'"

Revelation 5 v 7 - 13.

7. Holy, holy, holy, Lord God Almighty!

Holy, holy, holy, Lord God Almighty!
Early in the morning our song shall rise to Thee;
Holy, holy, holy, merciful and mighty,
God in Three Persons, blessed Trinity!

Holy, holy, holy! All the saints adore Thee,
Casting down their golden crowns around the glassy sea,
Cherubim and seraphim falling down before Thee,
Which wert, and art, and evermore shall be.

Holy, holy, holy! Though the darkness hide Thee,
Though the eye of sinful man Thy glory may not see,
Only Thou art holy; there is none beside Thee,
Perfect in power, in love, and purity.

Holy, holy, holy, Lord God Almighty!
All Thy works shall praise Thy name in earth
and sky and sea;
Holy, holy, holy, merciful and mighty,
God in Three Persons, blessed Trinity!

"The Lord Almighty is holy!"

"In the year that King Uzziah died, I saw the Lord. He was sitting on his throne, high and exalted, and his robe filled the whole Temple.

Round him flaming creatures were standing ... They were calling out to each other : 'Holy, holy, holy! The Lord Almighty is holy! His glory fills the world.'"

Isaiah 6 v 1 - 3.

"Lord, from the very beginning you are God. You are my God, holy and eternal... Your eyes are too holy to look at evil, and you cannot stand the sight of people doing wrong."

Habakkuk 1 v 12 - 13.

"If you kept a record of our sins, who could escape being condemned? But you forgive us, so that we should stand in awe of you."

Psalm 130 v 3 - 4.

"The Lord is merciful and loving, slow to become angry and full of constant love. He does not keep on rebuking; he is not angry for ever. He does not punish us as we deserve or repay us according to our sins and wrongs."

Psalm 103 v 8 - 10.

8. How Sweet the Name of Jesus sounds

How sweet the name of Jesus sounds
In a believer's ear!
It soothes his sorrows, heals his wounds,
And drives away his fear.

It makes the wounded spirit whole,
And calms the troubled breast;
'Tis manna to the hungry soul,
And to the weary rest.

Dear Name! The rock on which I build,
My shield and hiding place,
My never failing treasury, filled
With boundless stores of grace.

Jesus, my Shepherd, Husband, Friend,
My Prophet, Priest and King,
My Lord, my Life, my Way, my End,
Accept the praise I bring.

Weak is the effort of my heart,
And cold my warmest thought;
But when I see Thee as Thou art,
I'll praise Thee as I ought.

Till then I would Thy love proclaim
With every fleeting breath;
And may the music of Thy name
Refresh my soul in death.

"Praise the Lord"

"Praise the Lord, my soul! All my being, praise his holy name! Praise the Lord, my soul, and do not forget how kind he is. He forgives all my sins and heals all my diseases. He keeps me from the grave and blesses me with love and mercy."

Psalm 103 v 1 - 4.

"I always stay close to you, and you hold me by the hand. You guide me with your instruction and at the end you will receive me with honour. What else have I in heaven but you? Since I have you, what else could I want on earth? My mind and my body may grow weak, but God is my strength; he is all I ever need."

Psalm 73 v 23 - 26.

9. Immortal, invisible, God only wise

Immortal, invisible, God only wise,
In light inaccessible hid from our eyes,
Most blessed, most glorious, the Ancient of Days,
Almighty, victorious, Thy great Name we praise.

Unresting, unhasting, and silent as light,
Nor wanting, nor wasting, Thou rulest in might;
Thy justice, like mountains, high soaring above
Thy clouds which are fountains of goodness and love.

To all life Thou givest - to both great and small;
In all life Thou livest, the true life of all;
We blossom and flourish as leaves on the tree,
And wither and perish - but nought changeth Thee.

Great Father of Glory, pure Father of Light;
Thine angels adore Thee, all veiling their sight :
All laud we would render : O help us to see
'Tis only the splendour of light hideth Thee.

"His love lasts for ever"

"Strive for righteousness, godliness, faith, love, endurance, and gentleness. Run your best in the race of faith, and win eternal life for yourself; for it was to this life that God called you when you firmly professed your faith before many witnesses. Before God, who gives life to all things, and before Christ Jesus, who firmly professed his faith before Pontius Pilate, I command you to obey your orders and keep them faithfully until the Day when our Lord Jesus Christ will appear. His appearing will be brought about at the right time by God, the blessed and only ruler, the King of kings and the Lord of lords. He alone is immortal; he lives in the light that no one can approach. No one has ever seen him; no one can ever see him.

To him be honour and eternal dominion! Amen."

1 Timothy 6 v 11 - 16.

"We grow and flourish like a wild flower; then the wind blows on it and it is gone - no one sees it again. But for those who honour the Lord, his love lasts for ever, and his goodness endures for all generations of those who are true to his covenant and who faithfully obey his commands."

Psalm 103 v 15 - 18.

10. I need Thee every hour

I need Thee every hour,
Most gracious Lord;
No tender voice but Thine
Can peace afford.

> *I need Thee, O I need Thee;*
> *Every hour I need Thee*
> *O bless me now, my Saviour;*
> *I come to Thee.*

I need Thee every hour;
Stay Thou near by;
Temptations lose their power
When Thou art nigh.
> *I need Thee...*

I need Thee every hour,
In joy or pain;
Come quickly and abide
Or life is vain.
> *I need Thee...*

I need Thee every hour;
Teach me Thy will;
And Thy rich promises
In me fulfil.
> *I need Thee...*

"My grace is all you need"

"I was given a painful physical ailment, which acts as Satan's messenger to beat me and keep me from being proud. Three times I prayed to the Lord about this and asked him to take it away. But his answer was : 'My grace is all you need, for my power is greatest when you are weak.' I am most happy, then, to be proud of my weaknesses, in order to feel the protection of Christ's power over me. I am content with weaknesses, insults, hardships, persecutions, and difficulties for Christ's sake. For when I am weak, then I am strong.

2 Corinthians 12 v 7 - 10.

"I know what it is to be in need and what it is to have more than enough. I have learnt this secret, so that anywhere, at any time, I am content, whether I am full or hungry, whether I have too much or too little. I have the strength to face all conditions by the power that Christ gives me."

Philippians 4 v 12 - 13.

11. In the Cross of Christ I glory

In the Cross of Christ I glory,
Towering o'er the wrecks of time;
All the light of sacred story
Gathers round its head sublime.

When the woes of life o'ertake me,
Hopes deceive and fears annoy,
Never shall the Cross forsake me;
Lo! it glows with peace and joy.

When the sun of bliss is beaming
Light and love upon my way,
From the Cross the radiance streaming
Adds more lustre to the day.

Bane and blessing, pain and pleasure,
By the Cross are sanctified;
Peace is there that knows no measure,
Joys that through all time abide.

In the Cross of Christ I glory,
Towering o'er the wrecks of time;
All the light of sacred story
Gathers round its head sublime.

"The Crucified Christ"

"We proclaim the crucified Christ, a message that is offensive to the Jews and nonsense to the Gentiles; but for those whom God has called, both Jews and Gentiles, this message is Christ, who is the power of God and the wisdom of God."

1 Corinthians 1 v 23 - 24.

"Christ is the visible likeness of the invisible God. He is the first-born Son, superior to all created things. For through him God created everything in heaven and on earth, the seen and the unseen things, including spiritual powers, lords, rulers, and authorities. God created the whole universe through him and for him. Christ existed before all things, and in union with him all things have their proper place. He is the head of his body, the church; he is the source of the body's life. He is the first-born Son, who was raised from death, in order that he alone might have the first place in all things. For it was by God's own decision that the Son has in himself the whole nature of God. Through the Son, then, God decided to bring the whole universe back to himself. God made peace through his Son's sacrificial death on the cross and so brought back to himself all things, both on earth and in heaven."

Colossians 1 v 15 - 20.

12. Jesus, Lover of my soul

Jesus, Lover of my soul,
Let me to Thy bosom fly,
While the nearer waters roll,
While the tempest still is high;
Hide me, O my Saviour, hide
Till the storm of life be past;
Safe into the haven guide;
O receive my soul at last!

Other refuge have I none;
Hangs my helpless soul on Thee;
Leave, ah! leave me not alone;
Still support and comfort me.
All my trust on Thee is stayed;
All my help from Thee I bring;
Cover my defenceless head
With the shadow of Thy wing.

Thou, O Christ art all I want;
More than all in Thee I find;
Raise the fallen, cheer the faint,
Heal the sick, and lead the blind.
Just and holy is Thy name,
I am all unrighteousness;
False and full of sin I am,
Thou art full of truth and grace.

Plenteous grace with Thee is found,
Grace to cover all my sin;
Let the healing streams abound;
Make and keep me pure within.
Thou of life the fountain art,
Freely let me take of Thee;
Spring Thou up within my heart,
Rise to all eternity.

"Be merciful to me, O God"

"For God loved the world so much that he gave his only Son, so that everyone who believes in him may not die but have eternal life. For God did not send his Son into the world to be its judge, but to be its saviour."

John 3 v 16 - 17.

Jesus said, "I will never turn away anyone who comes to me."

John 6 v 37.

"Be merciful to me, O God, because of your constant love. Because of your great mercy wipe away all my sins! Wash away all my evil and make me clean from my sin!.. Remove my sin, and I will be clean; wash me, and I will be whiter than snow... Close your eyes to my sins and wipe out all my evil. Create a pure heart in me, O God, and put a new and loyal spirit in me. Do not banish me from your presence; do not take away your holy spirit from me. Give me again the joy that comes from your salvation, and make me willing to obey you."

Psalm 51 v 1 -2, 7, 9 - 12.

13. Jesus Christ is risen today

Jesus Christ is risen today,
      Hallelujah!
Our triumphant holy day,
      Hallelujah!
Who did once, upon the Cross,
      Hallelujah!
Suffer to redeem our loss.
      Hallelujah!

Hymns of praise, then, let us sing
Unto Christ, our heavenly King,
Who endured the Cross and grave,
Sinners to redeem and save.

But the anguish He endured
Our salvation hath procured;
Now above the skies He's King,
Where the angels ever sing.

Sing we to our God above
Praise eternal as His love;
Praise Him, all ye heavenly host,
Father, Son and Holy Ghost.

Christ has been raised from death

"I passed on to you what I received, which is of the greatest importance : that Christ died for our sins, as written in the Scriptures; that he was buried and that he was raised to life three days later, as written in the Scriptures...

The truth is that Christ has been raised from death, as the guarantee that those who sleep in death will also be raised. For just as death came by a man, in the same way the rising from death comes by means of a man. For just as all people die because of their union with Adam, in the same way all will be raised to life because of their union with Christ."

1 Corinthians 15 v 3 - 4 & 20 - 22.

"We do see Jesus, who for a little while was made lower than the angels, so that through God's grace he should die for everyone. We see him now crowned with glory and honour because of the death he suffered. It was only right that God, who creates and preserves all things, should make Jesus perfect through suffering, in order to bring many sons to share his glory. For Jesus is the one who leads them to salvation."

Hebrews 2 v 9 - 10.

14. Jesus loves me!

Jesus loves me! This I know,
For the Bible tells me so;
Little ones to Him belong;
They are weak, but He is strong.
Yes, Jesus loves me!
Yes, Jesus loves me!
Yes, Jesus loves me!
The Bible tells me so.

Jesus loves me! He who died
Heaven's gate to open wide;
He will wash away my sin,
Let His little child come in.
Yes, Jesus loves me...

Jesus loves me! He will stay
Close beside me all the way;
Then His little child will take
Up to heaven, for His dear sake.
Yes, Jesus loves me...

Jesus loves me!

"Some people brought their babies to Jesus for him to place his hands on them. The disciples saw them and scolded them for doing so, but Jesus called the children to him and said, 'Let the children come to me and do not stop them, because the kingdom of God belongs to such as these. Remember this! Whoever does not receive the Kingdom of God like a child will never enter it.'"

Luke 18 v 15 - 17.

"God has shown how much he loves us - it was while we were still sinners that Christ died for us."

Romans 5 v 8.

"'Do not be worried and upset,' Jesus told them. 'Believe in God and believe also in me. There are many rooms in my Father's house, and I am going to prepare a place for you. I would not tell you this if it were not so. And after I go and prepare a place for you, I will come back and take you to myself, so that you will be where I am.'"

John 14 v 1 - 3.

15. Jesus, Thou Joy of loving hearts

Jesus, Thou Joy of loving hearts,
Thou Fount of Life, Thou Light of men;
From the best bliss that earth imparts
We turn unfilled to Thee again.

Thy truth unchanged hath ever stood;
Thou savest those that on Thee call:
To them that seek Thee, Thou art good,
To them that find Thee, all in all.

We taste Thee, O Thou living Bread,
And long to feast upon Thee still;
We drink of Thee, the Fountain-head,
And thirst our souls from Thee to fill.

Our restless spirits yearn for Thee,
Where'er our changeful lot is cast, -
Glad when Thy gracious smile we see,
Blest when our faith can hold Thee fast.

O Jesus, ever with us stay;
Make all our moments calm and bright;
Chase the dark night of sin away;
Shed o'er the world Thy holy light.

"God's peace"

"Your word, O Lord, will last for ever; it is eternal in heaven. Your faithfulness endures through all the ages; you have set the earth in place and it remains. All things remain to this day because of your command, because they are all your servants."

Psalm 119 v 89 - 91.

"The peace that Christ gives is to guide you in the decisions you make; for it is to this peace that God has called you together in the one body. And be thankful. Christ's message in all its richness must live in your hearts. Teach and instruct each other with all wisdom. Sing psalms, hymns, and sacred songs; sing to God with thanksgiving in your hearts."

Colossians 3 v 15 - 17.

"Don't worry about anything, but in all your prayers ask God for what you need, always asking him with a thankful heart. And God's peace, which is far beyond human understanding, will keep your hearts and minds safe in union with Christ Jesus."

Philippians 4 v 6 - 7.

16. Just as I am

Just as I am, without one plea
But that Thy blood was shed
for me,
And that thou bidst me come
to Thee,
O Lamb of God, I come.

Just as I am, and waiting not
To rid my soul of one dark blot,
To Thee, whose blood can
cleanse each spot,
O Lamb of God, I come.

Just as I am, though tossed
about
With many a conflict, many a
doubt,
Fightings and fears, within,
without,
O Lamb of God, I come.

Just as I am, poor, wretched,
blind, -
Sight, riches, healing of the
mind,
Yea, all I need in Thee to find,
O Lamb of God, I come.

Just as I am, Thou wilt receive,
Wilt welcome, pardon,
cleanse, relieve;
Because Thy promise I
believe,
O Lamb of God, I come.

Just as I am, - Thy love
unknown
Has broken every barrier
down -
Now to be Thine, yea, Thine
alone,
O Lamb of God, I come.

Just as I am, of that free love
The breadth, length, depth
and height to prove,
Here for a season, then
above, -
O Lamb of God, I come.

"The God who forgives"

"The Lord says, 'I have swept your sins away like a cloud. Come back to me; I am the one who saves you.'"

Isaiah 44 v 22.

"The Lord says, 'I am the God who forgives your sins, and I do this because of who I am. I will not hold your sins against you.'"

Isaiah 43 v 25.

"Turn to the Lord and pray to him, now that he is near. Let the wicked leave their way of life and change their way of thinking. Let them turn to the Lord, our God; he is merciful and quick to forgive. "

Isaiah 55 v 6 - 7.

"Let us praise God for his glorious grace, for the free gift he gave us in his dear Son! For by the sacrificial death of Christ we are set free, that is, our sins are forgiven. How great is the grace of God, which he gave us in such large measure!"

Ephesians 1 v 6 - 8.

17. Love divine

Love divine, all loves excelling,
Joy of heaven to earth come down,
Fix in us Thy humble dwelling
All Thy faithful mercies crown.
Jesus, thou art all compassion
Pure, unbounded love Thou art;
Visit us with Thy salvation,
Enter every trembling heart.

Come, almighty to deliver;
Let us all Thy life receive;
Suddenly return, and never,
Never more Thy temples leave.
Thee we would be always blessing,
Serve Thee as Thy hosts above,
Pray, and praise Thee, without ceasing,
Glory in Thy perfect love.

Finish then Thy new creation;
Pure and spotless let us be;
Let us see Thy great salvation,
Perfectly restored in Thee.
Changed from glory into glory,
Till in heaven we take our place,
Till we cast our crowns before Thee,
Lost in wonder, love and praise.

"The knowledge of God's glory"

"The God who said, 'Out of darkness the light shall shine!' is the same God who made his light shine in our hearts, to bring us the knowledge of God's glory shining in the face of Christ."

2 Corinthians 4 v 6.

"We know that God, who raised the Lord Jesus to life, will also raise us up with Jesus and take us together with you, into his presence. All this is for your sake; and as God's grace reaches more and more people, they will offer to the glory of God more prayers of thanksgiving.

For this reason we never become discouraged. Even though our physical being is gradually decaying, yet our spiritual being is renewed day after day. And this small and temporary trouble we suffer will bring us a tremendous and eternal glory, much greater than the trouble. For we fix our attention, not on things that are seen, but on things that are unseen. What can be seen lasts only for a time, but what cannot be seen lasts for ever."

2 Corinthians 4 v 14 - 18.

18. Man of Sorrows!

Man of Sorrows! wondrous Name
For the Son of God, who came
Ruined sinners to reclaim!
Hallelujah! what a Saviour!

Bearing shame and scoffing rude,
In my place condemned He stood,
Sealed my pardon with His blood:
Hallelujah! what a Saviour!

Guilty, vile, and helpless we;
Spotless Lamb of God was He:
Full atonement, - can it be?
Hallelujah! what a Saviour!

Lifted up was He to die,
'It is finished' was His cry;
Now in heaven exalted high:
Hallelujah! what a Saviour!

When He comes, our glorious King,
All His ransomed home to bring,
Then anew this song we'll sing,
'Hallelujah! what a Saviour!'

"Because of our sins he was wounded"

"It was the will of the Lord that his servant should grow like a plant taking root in dry ground. He had no dignity or beauty to make us take notice of him. There was nothing attractive about him, nothing that would draw us to him. We despised and rejected him; he endured suffering and pain. No one would even look at him - we ignored him as if he were nothing.

But he endured the suffering that should have been ours, the pain that we should have borne. All the while we thought that his suffering was punishment sent from God. But because of our sins he was wounded, beaten because of the evil we did. We are healed by the punishment he suffered, made whole by the blows he received.

All of us were like sheep that were lost, each of us going his own way. But the Lord made the punishment fall on him, the punishment all of us deserved."

Isaiah 53 v 2 - 6.

19. My faith looks up to Thee

My faith looks up to Thee,
Thou Lamb of Calvary,
Saviour Divine :
Now hear me while I pray;
Take all my guilt away;
O let me from this day
Be wholly Thine.

May Thy rich grace impart
Strength to my fainting heart,
My zeal inspire;
As Thou hast died for me,
O may my love to Thee
Pure, warm, and changeless
be,
A living fire

While life's dark maze I tread,
And griefs around me spread,
Be thou my Guide;
Bid darkness turn to day,
Wipe sorrows tears away,
Nor let me ever stray
From Thee aside.

When ends life's transient
dream,
And death's cold, sullen
stream
Shall o'er me roll,
Blest Saviour, then in love
Fear and distrust remove;
O bear me safe above
A ransomed soul.

"I will be with you"

"The Lord who created you says,

'Do not be afraid - I will save you. I have called you by name - you are mine. When you pass through deep waters I will be with you; your troubles will not overwhelm you. When you pass through fire, you will not be burnt; the hard trials that come will not hurt you. For I am the Lord your God, the holy God of Israel who saves you.'"

Isaiah 43 v 1 - 3.

"Then I saw a new heaven and a new earth. The first heaven and the first earth disappeared, and the sea vanished. And I saw the holy city, the new Jerusalem, coming down out of heaven from God, prepared and ready, like a bride dressed to meet her husband. I heard a loud voice speaking from the throne: 'Now God's home is with mankind! He will live with them, and they shall be his people. He will wipe away all tears from their eyes. There will be no more death, no more grief or crying or pain. The old things have disappeared."

Revelation 21 v 1 - 4.

"Whoever wants to serve me must follow me, so that my servant will be with me where I am. "

John 12 v 26.

20. O Love that wilt not let me go

O Love that wilt not let me go,
I rest my weary soul in Thee :
I give Thee back the life I owe,
That in Thine ocean's depth its flow
May richer, fuller be.

O Light that followest all my way,
I yield my flickering torch to Thee :
My heart restores its borrowed ray,
That in Thy sunshine's blaze its day
May brighter, fairer be.

O Joy that seekest me through pain,
I cannot close my heart to Thee :
I trace the rainbow through the rain,
And feel the promise is not vain,
That morn shall tearless be.

O Cross that liftest up my head,
I dare not ask to fly from Thee :
I lay in dust life's glory dead,
And from the ground there blossoms red
Life that shall endless be.

"My constant love"

The Lord says, "I have always loved you, so I continue to show you my constant love."

Jeremiah 31 v 3.

"'Do not be worried and upset,' Jesus told them. 'Believe in God and believe also in me. There are many rooms in my Father's house, and I am going to prepare a place for you. I would not tell you this if were not so. And after I go and prepare a place for you, I will come back and take you to myself, so that you will be where I am."

John 14 v 1 - 3.

"When the kindness and love of God our Saviour was revealed, he saved us. It was not because of any good deeds that we ourselves had done, but because of his mercy that he saved us."

Titus 3 v 4 - 5.

"Jesus loves us, and by his sacrificial death he has freed us from our sins and made us a kingdom of priests to serve his God and Father. To Jesus Christ be the glory and power for ever and ever! Amen"

Revelation 1 v 6.

21. The old rugged Cross

On a hill far away stood an old rugged Cross,
the emblem of suffering and shame;
and I love that old Cross where the dearest and best
for a world of lost sinners was slain.
So I'll cherish the old rugged Cross
till my trophies at last I lay down;
I will cling to the old rugged Cross
and exchange it some day for a crown.

O, that old rugged Cross, so despised by the world,
has a wondrous attraction for me;
for the dear Lamb of God left His glory above
to bear it to dark Calvary.
So I'll cherish .....

In the old rugged Cross, stained with blood so divine,
a wondrous beauty I see;
for 'twas on that old Cross Jesus suffered and died
to pardon and sanctify me.
So I'll cherish .....

To the old rugged Cross I will ever be true,
its shame and reproach gladly bear;
then He'll call me some day to my home far away,
when His glory for ever I'll share.
So I'll cherish ....

"Our sins are forgiven."

"Give thanks to the Father, who has made you fit to have your share of what God has reserved for his people in the kingdom of light. He rescued us from the power of darkness and brought us safe into the kingdom of his dear Son, by whom we are set free, that is, our sins are forgiven."

Colossians 2 v 12 - 14.

"Our brothers, we want you to know the truth about those who have died, so that you will not be sad, as are those who have no hope. We believe that Jesus died and rose again, and so we believe that God will take back with Jesus those who have died believing in him.

What we are teaching you now is the Lord's teaching : we who are alive on the day the Lord comes will not go ahead of those who have died. There will be the shout of command, the archangel's voice, the sound of God's trumpet and the Lord himself will come down from heaven. Those who have died believing in Christ will rise to life first; then we who are living at that time will be gathered up along with them in the clouds to meet the Lord in the air. And so we will always be with the Lord. So then, encourage one another with these words."

1 Thessalonians 4 v 13 - 17.

22. Praise, my soul, the King of heaven

Praise, my soul, the King of heaven;
To His feet Thy tribute bring;
Ransomed, healed, restored, forgiven,
Who like me His praise should sing?
Praise Him! Praise Him!
Praise Him! Praise Him!
Praise the everlasting King.

Praise Him for His grace and favour
To our fathers in distress;
Praise Him still the same for ever,
Slow to chide and swift to bless:
Praise Him! Praise Him!
Praise Him! Praise Him!
Glorious in His faithfulness.

Father-like, He tends and spares us
Well our feeble frame He knows
In his hands He gently bears us,
Rescues us from all our foes:
Praise Him! Praise Him!
Praise Him! Praise Him!
Widely as His mercy flows.

Frail as summer's flower we flourish
Blows the wind and it is gone;
But, while mortals rise and perish,
God endures unchanging on:
Praise Him! Praise Him!
Praise Him! Praise Him!
Praise the high eternal One.

Angels, help us to adore Him;
Ye behold Him face to face;
Sun and moon, bow down before Him;
Dwellers all in time and space,
Praise Him! Praise Him!
Praise Him! Praise Him!
Praise with us the God of grace.

"Do not start worrying"

Jesus said, "Do not store up riches for yourselves here on earth, where moths and rust destroy, and robbers break in and steal. Instead, store up riches for yourselves in heaven... For your heart will always be where your riches are...

"This is why I tell you not to be worried about the food and drink you need to stay alive, or about clothes for your body. After all, isn't the body worth more than food? And isn't the body worth more than clothes? Look at the birds : they do not sow seeds, gather a harvest, and put it in barns; yet your Father in heaven takes care of them! Aren't you worth much more than birds? Can you live a bit longer by worrying about it?...

"So do not start worrying : 'Where will my food come from? or my drink? or my clothes?' (These are all the things the pagans are always concerned about.) Your Father in heaven knows that you need all these things. Instead, be concerned above everything else with the Kingdom of God and with what he requires of you, and he will provide you with all these other things. So do not worry about tomorrow; it will have enough worries of its own. There is no need to add to the troubles each day brings."

Matthew 6 v 19 - 21, 25 - 27, & 28 - 34.

23. Ride on! ride on in majesty!

Ride on! ride on in majesty!
Hark! all the tribes 'Hosanna' cry;
O Saviour meek, pursue thy road
With palms and scattered garments strowed.

Ride on! ride on in majesty!
In lowly pomp ride on to die;
O Christ, Thy triumphs now begin
O'er captive death and conquered sin.

Ride on! ride on in majesty!
The winged squadrons of the sky
Look down with sad and wondering eyes
To see the approaching sacrifice.

Ride on! ride on in majesty!
Thy last and fiercest strife is nigh;
The Father on His sapphire throne
Awaits His own annointed Son.

Ride on! ride on in majesty!
In lowly pomp ride on to die;
Bow Thy meek head to mortal pain,
Then take, O God, Thy power, and reign.

"The triumphant Lord"

"John saw Jesus coming to him, and said, 'There is the Lamb of God, who takes away the sin of the world... I tell you that he is the Son of God.'"

John 1 v 29 & 34.

"Pilate's soldiers took Jesus into the governor's palace, and the whole company gathered round him. They stripped off his clothes and put a scarlet robe on him. Then they made a crown out of thorny branches and placed it on his head, and put a stick in his right hand; then they knelt before him and mocked him. 'Long live the King of the Jews!' they said. They spat on him, and took the stick and hit him over the head. When they had finished mocking him, they took the robe off and put his own clothes back on him. Then they led him out to crucify him."

Matthew 27 v 27 - 30.

"Fling wide the gates, open the ancient doors, and the great king will come in. Who is this great king? He is the Lord, strong and mighty, the Lord, victorious in battle.

Fling wide the gates, open the ancient doors, and the great king will come in. Who is this great king? The triumphant Lord - he is the great king!"

Psalm 24 v 7 - 10.

24. Rock of Ages

Rock of Ages, cleft for me,
Let me hide myself in Thee;
Let the water and the blood,
From Thy riven side which flowed,
Be of sin the double cure,
Cleanse me from its guilt and power.

Not the labours of my hands
Can fulfill Thy law's demands;
Could my zeal no respite know,
Could my tears for ever flow,
All for sin could not atone:
Thou must save, and Thou alone.

Nothing in my hand I bring,
Simply to Thy Cross I cling;
Naked, come to Thee for dress;
Helpless, look to Thee for grace;
Foul, I to the fountain fly;
Wash me, Saviour, or I die.

While I draw this fleeting breath,
When mine eyelids close in death,
When I soar through tracts unknown,
See Thee on Thy judgement throne,
Rock of Ages, cleft for me,
Let me hide myself in Thee.

"Nothing can separate us from his love"

Jesus also told this parable to people who were sure of their own goodness and despised everybody else.

"Once there were two men who went up to the temple to pray : one was a Pharisee, the other a tax collector.

"The Pharisee stood apart by himself and prayed, 'I thank you, God, that I am not greedy, dishonest, or an adulterer, like everybody else. I thank you that I am not like that tax collector over there. I fast two days a week, and I give you a tenth of all my income.'

"But the tax collector stood at a distance and would not even raise his face to heaven, but beat on his breast and said, 'God, have pity on me, a sinner!' I tell you," said Jesus, "the tax collector, not the Pharisee, was in the right with God when he went home. For everyone who makes himself great will be humbled, and everyone who humbles himself will be made great."

Luke 18 v 9 - 14.

"For I am certain that nothing can separate us from his love : neither death, nor life, neither angels nor other heavenly rulers or powers, neither the world above nor the world below - there is nothing in all creation that will ever be able to separate us from the love of God which is ours through Christ Jesus our Lord."

Romans 8 v 38 - 39.

25. The Lord's my Shepherd

The Lord's my Shepherd, I'll not want.
He makes me down to lie
in pastures green : He leadeth me
the quiet waters by.

My soul He doth restore again;
and me to walk doth make
within the paths of righteousness,
e'en for His own Name's sake

Yea, though I walk in death's dark vale,
yet will I fear none ill :
for Thou art with me; and Thy rod
and staff me comfort still.

My table thou hast furnished
in presence of my foes;
my head Thou dost with oil annoint,
and my cup overflows.

Goodness and mercy all my life
shall surely follow me :
and in God's house for evermore
my dwelling place shall be.

"The good shepherd"

"As Jesus saw the crowds, his heart was filled with pity for them, because they were worried and helpless, like sheep without a shepherd."

Matthew 9 v 36.

"Come, let us bow down and worship him; let us kneel before the Lord, our Maker! He is our God; we are the people he cares for, the flock for which he provides."

Psalm 95 v 6 - 7.

Jesus said, "I am the good shepherd, who is willing to die for the sheep... I am the good shepherd. As my Father knows me and I know the Father, in the same way I know my sheep and they know me. There are other sheep that belong to me that are not of this sheepfold. I must bring them, too; they will listen to my voice, and they will become one flock with one shepherd.

"The Father loves me because I am willing to give up my life, in order that I may receive it back again. No one takes my life from me. I give it up of my own free will. I have the right to give it up, and I have the right to take it again. This is what my Father has commanded me to do."

John 10 v 11 & 14 - 18.

26. There is a green hill

There is a green hill far away,
Without a city wall,
Where the dear Lord was crucified,
Who died to save us all.

We may not know, we cannot tell
What pains He had to bear;
But we believe it was for us
He hung and suffered there.

He died that we might be forgiven,
He died to make us good,
That we might go at last to heaven
Saved by His precious blood.

There was no other good enough
To pay the price of sin;
He only could unlock the gate
Of heaven, and let us in.

O dearly, dearly has He loved,
And we must love Him too,
And trust in His redeeming blood,
And try His works to do.

"They crucified Jesus"

"When they came to the place called 'The Skull', they crucified Jesus there, and the two criminals, one on his right and the other on his left. Jesus said, 'Forgive them, Father! They don't know what they are doing.'

They divided his clothes among themselves by throwing dice. The people stood there watching while the Jewish leaders jeered at him : 'He saved others; let him save himself if he is the Messiah whom God has chosen!'...

One of the criminals hanging there hurled insults at him: 'Aren't you the Messiah? Save yourself and us!'

The other one, however, rebuked him, saying, 'Don't you fear God? You received the same sentence he did. Ours, however, is only right, because we are getting what we deserve for what we did; but he has done no wrong.' And he said to Jesus, 'Remember me, Jesus, when you come as King!'

Jesus said to him, 'I promise you that today you will be in paradise with me.'"

Luke 23 v 33 -35 & 39 - 43.

27. To God be the glory!

To God be the glory! great things He has done;
so loved He the world that He gave us His Son;
who yielded His life an atonement for sin,
and opened the life-gate that all may go in.
    Praise the Lord! Praise the Lord!
    Let the earth hear his voice;
    Praise the Lord! Praise the Lord!
    Let the people rejoice :
    O come to the Father through Jesus the Son
    and give Him the glory; great things He hath done.

O perfect redemption, the purchase of blood!
to every believer the promise of God;
the vilest offender who truly believes,
that moment from Jesus a pardon receives.
    Praise the Lord! ....

Great things He hath taught us, great things He hath done,
and great our rejoicing through Jesus the Son;
but purer, and higher, and greater will be
our wonder, our rapture, when Jesus we see.
    Praise the Lord! ....

"I offer peace to all"

"After Jesus had finished saying this, he looked up to heaven and said, 'Father the hour has come. Give glory to your Son, so that the Son may give glory to you. For you gave him authority over all mankind, so that he might give eternal life to all those you gave him. And eternal life means knowing you, the only true God, and Jesus Christ, whom you sent. I have shown your glory on earth; I have finished the work you gave me to do. Father! Give me glory in your presence now, the same glory I had with you before the world was made.'"

John 17 v 1 - 5.

"The Lord says, 'Let my people return to me. Remove every obstacle from their path! Build the road, and make it ready! I am the high and holy God, who lives for ever. I live in a high and holy place, but I also live with people who are humble and repentant, so that I may restore their confidence and hope...

'I will heal them. I will lead them and help them, and I will comfort those that mourn. I offer peace to all, both near and far! I will heal my people.'"

Isaiah 57 v 14, 15, 18 & 19.

28. Today Thy mercy calls us

Today Thy mercy calls us
To wash away our sin,
However great our trespass,
Whatever we have been;
How ever long from mercy
We may have turned away,
Thy blood, O Christ, can cleanse us,
And make us white today.

Today Thy gate is open,
And all who enter in
Shall find a Father's welcome,
And pardon for their sin;
The past shall be forgotten,
A present joy be given,
A future grace be promised,
A glorious crown in heaven.

O all-embracing mercy,
Thou ever-open Door,
What should we do without Thee
When heart and eye run o'er?
When all things seem against us,
To drive us to despair,
We know one gate is open,
One ear will hear our prayer

"I have sinned"

Jesus went on to say, "There was once a man who had two sons. The younger one said to him, 'Father, give me my share of the property now.' So the man divided his property between his two sons. After a few days the younger son sold his part of the property and left home with the money. He went to a country far away, where he wasted his money in reckless living. He spent everything he had. Then a severe famine spread over that country, and he was left without a thing. So he went to work for one of the citizens of that country, who sent him out into his farm to take care of the pigs. He wished he could fill himself with the bean pods the pigs ate, but no one gave him anything to eat. At last he came to his senses and said, 'All my father's hired workers have more than they can eat, and here I am about to starve! I will get up and go to my father and say, Father, I have sinned against God and against you. I am no longer fit to be called your son; treat me as one of your hired workers.' So he got up and started back to his father.

"He was still a long way from home when his father saw him; his heart was filled with pity, and he ran, threw his arms round his son, and kissed him. 'Father,' the son said, 'I have sinned against God and against you. I am no longer fit to be called your son.' But the father called his servants. 'Hurry!' he said. 'Bring the best robe and put it on him. Put a ring on his finger and shoes on his feet. Then go and get the prize calf and kill it, and let us celebrate with a feast! For this son of mine was dead, but now he is alive; he was lost, but now he has been found.'

Luke 15 v 11 - 24.

29. We sing the praise of Him who died

We sing the praise of Him who died,
Of Him who died upon the Cross;
The sinner's hope let men deride,
For this we count the world but loss.

Inscribed upon the Cross we see,
In shining letters, 'God is love';
He bears our sins upon the Tree;
He brings us mercy from above.

The Cross! it takes our guilt away;
It holds the fainting spirit up;
It cheers with hope the gloomy day,
And sweetens every bitter cup;

It makes the coward spirit brave,
It nerves the feeble arm for fight;
It takes its terror from the grave,
And gilds the bed of death with light;

The balm of life, the cure of woe,
The measure and the pledge of love,
The sinners' refuge here below,
The angels' theme in heaven above.

"Christ died for us!"

"God puts people right through their faith in Jesus Christ. God does this to all who believe in Christ, because there is no difference at all: everyone has sinned and is far away from God's saving presence. But all are put right with him through Christ Jesus, who sets them free. God offered him, so that by his sacrificial death he should become the means by which people's sins are forgiven through their faith in him."

Romans 3 v 23 - 25.

"For while we were still helpless, Christ died for the wicked at the time God chose. It is a difficult thing for someone to die for a righteous person. It may even be that someone might dare to die for a good person. But God has shown us how much he loves us - it was while we were still sinners that Christ died for us!"

Romans 5 v 6 - 8.

"God saved us and called us to be his own people, not because of what we have done, but because of his own purpose and grace. He gave this grace to us by means of Christ Jesus before the beginning of time, but now it has been revealed to us through the coming of our Saviour, Christ Jesus. He has ended the power of death and through the Gospel has revealed immortal life."

2 Timothy 1 v 9 - 10.

30. What a friend we have in Jesus

What a friend we have in Jesus,
All our sins and griefs to bear!
What a privilege to carry
Everything to God in prayer!
O what peace we often forfeit,
O what needless pain we bear,
All because we do not carry
Everything to God in prayer!

Have we trials and temptations?
Is there trouble anywhere?
We should never be discouraged :
Take it to the Lord in prayer!
Can we find a friend so faithful,
Who will all our sorrows share?
Jesus knows our every weakness :
Take it to the Lord in prayer.

Are we weak and heavy-laden,
Cumbered with a load of care?
Jesus only is our refuge :
Take it to the Lord in prayer.
Do Thy friends despise, forsake thee?
Take it to the Lord in prayer;
In His arms He'll take and shield thee;
Thou wilt find a solace there.

"Don't worry about anything"

"May you always be joyful in your union with the Lord. I say it again : rejoice! Show a gentle attitude to everyone. The Lord is coming soon. Don't worry about anything, but in all your prayers ask God for what you need, always asking him with a thankful heart. And God's peace, which is far beyond human understanding, will keep your hearts and minds safe in union with Christ Jesus."

Philippians 4 v 4 - 7.

"Do not be afraid, little flock, for your Father is pleased to give you the Kingdom."

Luke 12 v 32 .

"Come to me, all of you who are tired from carrying heavy loads, and I will give you rest. Take my yoke and put it on you, and learn from me, because I am gentle and humble in spirit; and you will find rest. For the yoke I will give you is easy, and the load I will put on you is light."

Matthew 11 v 28 - 30.

31. When I survey the wondrous cross

When I survey the wondrous cross
On which the Prince of Glory died,
My richest gain I count but loss,
And pour contempt on all my pride.

Forbid it, Lord, that I should boast,
Save in the death of Christ, my God;
All the vain things that charm me most,
I sacrifice them to His blood.

See! from His head, His hands, His feet,
Sorrow and love flow mingled down;
Did e'er such love and sorrow meet,
Or thorns compose so rich a crown?

Were the whole realm of nature mine,
That were an offering far too small;
Love so amazing, so divine,
Demands my soul, my life, my all.

"He loved us"

"God showed his love for us by sending his only Son into the world, so that we might have life through him. This is what love is : it is not that we have loved God, but that he loved us and sent his Son to be the means by which our sins are forgiven."

1 John 4 v 9 - 10.

"So then, my brothers, because of God's great mercy to us I appeal to you : Offer yourselves as a living sacrifice to God, dedicated to his service and pleasing to him. This is the true worship you should offer. Do not conform yourselves to the standards of this world, but let God transform you inwardly by a complete change of your mind. Then you will be able to know the will of God - what is good and is pleasing to him and is perfect."

Romans 12 v 1 - 3.

"To him who is able to keep you from falling, and bring you faultless before his glorious presence - to the only God our Saviour, through Christ Jesus our Lord, be glory, majesty, might, and authority, from all ages past, and now, and for ever and ever! Amen."

Jude 24 - 25.

First Line	Tune	CH3*	MP**
1. Abide with me	Eventide	695	4
2. Amazing grace	Amazing grace		31
3. At the name of Jesus	Camberwell		41
	Cuddeston	300	
4. Beneath the cross of Jesus	St Christopher		55
5. Come, Holy Spirit, come	Franconia	104	
6. Crown Him with many crowns	Diademata	298	109
7. Holy, holy, holy,	Nicea	352	237
8. How sweet the name of Jesus	St Peter	376	251
9. I need Thee every hour	Bread of Life	687	
	I need Thee		288
10. Immortal, invisible, God only wise	St Denoi (Joanna)	32	327
11. In the Cross of Christ I glory	Stuttgart	259	
	St Oswald		338
12. Jesus Lover of my soul	Aberystwyth	78	372
	Hollingside	78	
13. Jesus Christ is risen today	Easter Hymn	264	
	Llanfair		357
14. Jesus loves me	Gaelic Lullaby	418	
	Jesus loves me	418	
15. Jesus, Thou Joy of loving hearts	Maryton		383
	Wareham	571	
16. Just as I am	Woodworth		396
	Misericordia		396
	Saffron Walden	79	
17. Love Divine	Blaenwern	473	449
	Hyfrydol	437	
18. Man of Sorrows	Gethsemane	380	458
19. My faith looks up	Olivet	81	469
20. O Love that wilt not let me go	St Margaret	677	515
21. On a hill far away	The Old Rugged Cross		536
22. Praise, my soul	Praise, my soul	360	560
23. Ride on, ride on	St Drostane		580
	Winchester New	234	
24. Rock of Ages	Petra	83	582
	Toplady		582
25. The Lord's my Shepherd	Crimond	387	660
	Wiltshire	387	
26. There is a green hill	Horsley	241	674
27. To God be the glory	To God be the glory	708	
28. Today Thy mercy calls us	Penlan	681	331
29. We sing the praise of Him	Warrington	738	
	Walton (Fulda)	258	
30. What a friend we have in Jesus	Converse		746
31. When I survey the wondrous Cross	Rockingham	254	755

* Church Hymnary Third Edition ** Mission Praise Combined Music Edition